The Art of Conversation:

Mastering the Skill of Talking to Women at 25"

Allan .R Thompson

Table of content

Introduction: The Importance of Effective Communication in Romantic Relationships

We all have been there - standing in a congested room, surrounded by friends and acquaintances, and yet unable to initiate a conversation with a woman we are attracted to. For many males, confronting a woman they find attractive can be an intimidating experience, and it often feels like the stakes are high. After all, a lot is depending on that first impression. Will she find us fascinating or awkward? Will she want to continue the conversation, or will she respectfully make an excuse to move away?

It's not just our dignity on the line, either. Effective communication is the cornerstone of any successful intimate relationship. From the early phases of flirtation and courtship to the later stages of establishing a long-term relationship, being able to communicate successfully is important. Misunderstandings, miscommunications, and wounded emotions can rapidly lead to the disintegration of even the strongest relationships.

That's why this guide is here to assist. Whether you're beginning to date for the first time or are seeking to enhance your existing communication skills, this guide will provide you with the tools and strategies you need to communicate confidently, successfully, and passionately with the women you encounter. But before we delve into the nitty-gritty, let me share with you a narrative of my own personal experience with communication.

I remember the first time I met my now-wife, Sarah. We were both in college, and I was at a gathering with a bunch of acquaintances. She grabbed my attention as soon as she strolled in the door, but I hesitated to approach her. I was apprehensive, uncertain of what to begin or how to initiate a conversation. As the night dragged on, I watched as other males made their way over to speak to her, and I chastised myself for not taking the opportunity.

It wasn't until later that night, as we were all departing the celebration, that I eventually gathered up the confidence to speak to her. And you know what? It was a catastrophe. I stammered over my words, said something foolish, and watched as she swiftly walked away. I was humiliated.

But I didn't give up. I knew I wanted to get to know her better, and so I made a commitment to improving my communication abilities. Over time, I learned how to approach women with confidence, how to keep a conversation moving, and how to interpret non-verbal signals. And ultimately, I captured Sarah's heart.

If I can do it, so can you. With the assistance of this guide, you can learn the skills you need to approach women with confidence and establish strong, healthy relationships through effective communication. So, let's get started

Chapter 1: Building Confidence and Overcoming Shyness

I know what it's like to feel bashful and apprehensive around people you're attracted to. It's a typical occurrence, and it can be a significant obstacle to establishing intimate relationships. But the good news is that confidence is something that can be acquired and maintained. In this chapter, we'll examine some practical techniques for developing confidence and conquering timidity so that you can approach ladies with comfort and confidence.

Embracing Your Unique Personality
One of the greatest blunders males make when attempting to attract a woman is to try to be someone they're not. Maybe you believe you need to appear more extroverted or confident than you really are, or maybe you attempt to present an image that you think will make you

more attractive. But here's the thing: ladies can identify a phony from a mile away. If you're not being truthful to yourself, you'll come across as dishonest and untrustworthy.

Instead of attempting to be someone you're not, concentrate on accepting your distinct personality. Recognize that you have strengths and limitations and that there are people out there who will appreciate you for who you are. Being comfortable in your own flesh is an attractive characteristic, and it will help you develop confidence in your relationships with women.

But the reality is, there are plenty of women out there who appreciate a man who is contemplative, introspective, and independent. Instead of attempting to be the center of the party, you can appreciate your distinct personality and use it to your advantage.

For example, if you're at a social gathering and feeling overwhelmed, you can approach a woman and initiate a conversation about the novel you're presently reading. This can be a wonderful method to show off your intellectual side and to discover common ground with someone who shares your interests.

By accepting your distinct personality, you're able to be more authentic and sincere in your relationships with women. You don't have to attempt to be someone you're not, and you'll attract women who appreciate you for who you are. And that's the cornerstone of any robust, thriving relationship

Overcoming the Fear of Rejection
One of the greatest impediments to approaching women is the dread of rejection. Nobody wants to be rejected, and it can be a setback to your self-esteem. But the reality is, rejection is a typical aspect of the courting process. Not every woman is going to be interested in you, and that's alright.

To surmount the dread of rejection, it's essential to rethink how you think about it. Instead of watching

rejection as a personal failing, strive to see it as an opportunity to learn and develop. Maybe the woman you confronted wasn't a suitable match for you, or maybe you could have done something differently to create a better impression. By viewing rejection as a learning experience, you'll be able to recover back more swiftly and approach the next woman with more confidence.

To surmount this anxiety, you resolve to challenge yourself by confronting a woman you find attractive. You introduce yourself and initiate up a conversation, and although it's a bit uncomfortable at first, you're able to keep the conversation running. You invite her out on a date, but unfortunately, she declines.

At first, you feel disappointed and a little embarrassed. But instead of focusing on the rejection, you choose to concentrate on the positive elements of the relationship. You recognize that you were able to approach a woman you considered attractive and initiate up a conversation, something you would have never done before. You also understand that rejection is a typical part of the relationship process and that not every woman is going to be interested in you.

By interpreting the rejection as a learning experience, you're able to move on more swiftly and approach the next woman with more confidence. And who knows, maybe the next woman you approach will say yes and you'll have the opportunity to establish a significant relationship.

Developing a Positive Mindset
Finally, establishing an optimistic attitude is essential for building confidence and conquering timidity. Our thoughts have a significant influence on our feelings and behaviors, and

pessimistic self-talk can hold us back from accomplishing our objectives.

Instead of concentrating on all the things that could go wrong, attempt to concentrate on the advantages. Maybe you have a wonderful sense of comedy, or you're an excellent listener. By concentrating on your abilities, you'll be better prepared to approach women with confidence and charisma.

To cultivate a more optimistic attitude, you start by confronting your pessimistic self-talk. You understand that your thoughts have a significant influence on your feelings and behaviors and that by altering your thinking, you can transform your existence.

So the next time you're feeling down on yourself, you make a deliberate effort to concentrate on the positive elements of your existence. Maybe you have a wonderful collection of companions who adore and support you, or maybe you're flourishing in your profession. By concentrating on the positives, you're able to change your attitude and feel more confident and enthusiastic.

As you continue to exercise this new way of thinking, you start to observe a difference in your behavior. You begin to approach women with more confidence and charisma, and you start to establish stronger relationships with them. You recognize that your optimistic attitude is not only attractive to women, but it's also enabling you to live a more satisfying and successful existence.

By concentrating on the advantages and establishing a more optimistic mentality, you're able to build more confidence, overcome your timidity, and create the kind of life and relationships you genuinely want.

In the next chapter, we'll examine the power of attentive listening and how it can help you establish stronger relationships with women.

Chapter 2: The Power of Active Listening

It was a Friday evening, and I had arranged to meet up with a woman I had been seeing for a few weeks. We had decided to try a new establishment in town, and I was thrilled to see her.

As soon as we sat down, I launched into a narrative about my day at work, scarcely taking a breath as I described every detail. I was so concentrated on impressing her and making her giggle that I didn't even notice the dreamy expression in her eyes.

It wasn't until later in the evening, when she was telling me about her own day, that I recognized my blunder. As she spoke, I found myself only half-listening, my thoughts wandering to other topics. I was so concentrated on what I was going to say next that I didn't fully hear her remarks.

That night was a wake-up call for me. I recognized that if I wanted to establish a genuine relationship with this woman (or anyone, for that matter), I needed to become a better listener.

In this chapter, we'll examine the skill of listening and why it's so essential for establishing powerful, significant relationships. Whether you're on a first date or in a long-term relationship, learning to be a good listener can help you communicate with your companion on a deeper level and establish a more satisfying collaboration. So, let's plunge in.

As humans, we all have a deep-seated yearning to be heard and understood. We want to feel like our opinions, emotions, and experiences are legitimate and that someone is really listening to us. And that's where the skill of listening comes in.

Being a good observer means more than just nodding along as someone speaks. It means actively interacting with them, asking questions, and demonstrating sensitivity and comprehension. When you're a good listener, you're able to establish a secure and encouraging place for your companion to open up and share their innermost thoughts and emotions.

On the other hand, when you're a poor listener, you may unintentionally close your companion down or make them feel like their experiences aren't essential. This can lead to feelings of loneliness and disconnection, and can eventually damage your relationship.

So, how can you become a better listener?

Tips for Becoming a Better Listener

Put aside distractions. When you're having a conversation with someone, put aside your phone, switch off the TV, and eradicate any other interruptions. This tells the other person that you respect their time and that you're completely present in the situation.

Focus on the speaker. When someone is chatting to you, establish eye contact and really concentrate on what they're saying. Avoid allowing your thoughts to meander or preparing what you're going to say next. Instead, observe and participate in the conversation.

Ask inquiries. Asking inquiries can help you acquire a better comprehension of what the other person is saying and can also show them that you're attentive. Try to pose open-ended inquiries that encourage the speaker to elucidate and share more.

Show understanding. When someone is sharing their experiences or emotions with you, attempt to place yourself in their position and demonstrate sensitivity. This can help them feel acknowledged and understood.

Understanding the Art of Listening
Listening is an important ability that can help you create stronger relationships and strengthen

your interactions with others. To fully comprehend the skill of listening, it's essential to acknowledge that it's about more than just hearing what someone is saying. It's about constantly interacting with them, demonstrating sensitivity, and providing a secure place for them to express their innermost thoughts and emotions.

At its heart, listening includes three primary components: concentration, interpretation, and reaction. Here's a better look at each one:

Attention: To be an effective listener, you need to be completely present at the moment and offer the speaker your unwavering attention. This means putting aside any interruptions, establishing eye contact, and concentrating on what they're saying.

Interpretation: Once you're listening, you need to comprehend and understand what the speaker is saying. This includes not just hearing the words, but also giving attention to their body language, tone, and other behavioral signals.

Response: Finally, a crucial component of listening is responding to the speaker in a manner that demonstrates you comprehend and care about what they're saying. This can involve asking questions, demonstrating concern, or simply reflecting on what you've heard to make sure you're on the same page.

By understanding these three components of attention, you can start developing stronger, more significant relationships with the people in your life. Whether you're on a first date or in a long-term relationship, learning to be a good listener can help you communicate with your companion on a deeper level and establish a more satisfying collaboration. So, the next time you're having a conversation with someone, remember to be completely present, understand their words and behavioral signals, and respond in a manner that demonstrates your care.

Asking Open-Ended Questions?

One of the best methods to demonstrate that you're attentive and involved in a conversation is to pose open-ended inquiries. These are inquiries that can't be responded to with a straightforward "yes" or "no," but instead challenge the speaker to elucidate and share more. By asking open-ended inquiries, you're demonstrating that you're interested in the other person's thoughts and emotions and that you're committed to establishing a deeper relationship.

Here are some guidelines for asking open-ended questions:

Start with "What," "How," or "Why": These question starters can help you prevent closed-ended inquiries that can be responded to with a straightforward "yes" or "no." For example, instead of saying "Did you like the movie?" you could ask "What did you think of the movie?"

Follow up with a related question: Once the speaker has addressed your first question, follow up with another connected question to keep the conversation continuing. This demonstrates that you're constantly involved in the conversation and interested in what they have to say.

Avoid deceptive questions: Try to prevent inquiries that bring the speaker to a particular response. For example, instead of saying "Don't you think that was a great movie?" question "What did you think of the movie?"

Be genuine: Finally, consider that asking open-ended inquiries is about more than just following an algorithm. It's about demonstrating a sincere interest in the other individual and being prepared to listen to their thoughts and emotions.

Responding with Empathy
Responding with sensitivity is one of the most essential abilities in any communication. It includes genuinely comprehending and

acknowledging the other person's emotions, and responding in a manner that demonstrates you care. When you respond with empathy, you're establishing confidence and demonstrating to the other individual that you respect their feelings and experiences.

Here are some suggestions for responding with empathy:
Validate their feelings: One of the most essential things you can do is acknowledge the other person's emotions. This means understanding and embracing their feelings, even if you don't concur with them. For example, you might respond "I can understand why you're feeling upset right now."

Show understanding: When you respond with empathy, you're attempting to see things from the other person's perspective. Try to place yourself in their position and comprehend what they're going through. You might remark "I can see why you would feel that way."

Express concern: Responding with empathy is also about demonstrating that you care about the other individual. You might reply "I'm sorry you're going through this" or "Is there anything I can do to help?"

Avoid providing guidance: Finally, when responding with sensitivity, it's essential to avoid giving unwarranted advice. Instead, concentrate on listening and comprehending the other person's emotions.

When my acquaintance came to me and told me that he was feeling really down. He had just gone through a divorce and was struggling to deal with his feelings. I could see the anguish and despair in his gaze and realized that I needed to respond with understanding.

I started by acknowledging his emotions. "I'm so sorry that you're feeling this way," I said. "Breakups can be really tough."

Then, I attempted to demonstrate that I comprehend what he was going through. "I can imagine that this is really difficult for you," I said. "It's normal to feel sad and hurt after a breakup."

I also expressed concern and inquired if there was anything I could do to assist. "If you ever need someone to talk to, I'm here for you," I said.

By responding with sensitivity, I was able to demonstrate to my friend that I cared about his emotions and was there to support him. It made a genuine difference in his emotional condition, and we were able to have a deeper, more meaningful conversation about what he was going through.

Chapter 3: Conversation Starters and Icebreakers

I used to be incredibly timid when it came to beginning conversations with strangers. I was always concerned about speaking the incorrect thing or not knowing what to chat about. But I recognized that if I wanted to make new acquaintances and establish new relationships, I needed to burst out of my isolation.

So, one day I decided to attend a neighborhood networking gathering. I was apprehensive at first, but I realized that I needed to take the first move if I wanted to establish new relationships. As soon as I stepped in, I saw a woman who appeared pleasant and approachable. I decided to use a conversation starter and complimented her on her jewelry. She beamed and thanked me, and we started speaking about where she got it.

From there, the conversation proceeded effortlessly. We chatted about our careers, our interests, and even some amusing anecdotes. I discovered that the more I opened up and shared about myself, the simpler it was for her to do the same. By the conclusion of the gathering, we had exchanged phone information and made arrangements to get together again.

This experience showed me that beginning a conversation doesn't have to be frightening or intimidating. With a few straightforward conversation starters and icebreakers, you can break the ice and start establishing significant relationships with new people

One of the greatest difficulties when chatting with someone new is beginning the conversation. You might be concerned about speaking the incorrect thing or not understanding what to chat about. But with a few straightforward conversation starters and icebreakers, you can break the ice and get the conversation rolling.

Here are a few conversation starters and icebreakers to try:

commend them: Everyone adores a sincere commendation. Try beginning the conversation with a compliment about something they're wearing, their smile, or their employment. For example, you might respond "I love your shirt, where did you get it?"

Ask for their opinion: People adore expressing their thoughts and opinions. Ask them for their perspective on a current occurrence or something you're interested in. For example, you might state "What do you think about the latest Marvel movie?"

Talk about common interests: If you know the individual has a similar interest with you, use that as a conversation beginning. For example, if you both adore photography, you might remark "I noticed you have a camera, do you enjoy taking photos?"

Use an entertaining fact: Start the conversation with an enjoyable truth about yourself or something fascinating you've read recently. For example, you might say "Did you know that the world's largest pizza was 131 feet in diameter?"

Ask an open-ended question: As discussed in chapter 2, asking open-ended questions is a wonderful method to initiate a conversation. Ask them something that can't be responded to with a straightforward "yes" or "no." For example, you might say "What did you do over the weekend?"

Breaking the Ice with Humor

Using comedy can be an effective way to break the ice and place people at ease. However, it's essential to use comedy in a manner that's appropriate and considerate.

I remember a moment when I was at a social gathering and didn't recognize anyone in the room. I felt apprehensive and uncertain about how to initiate a conversation. However, I decided to attempt to use comedy to break the ice.

I overheard a gathering of people chatting about their favorite movies, and one individual mentioned a movie that I hadn't seen. I made a jest about being behind on my movie-watching and said "I'm still stuck in the 90s!" This garnered a few chuckles and led to a conversation about some of our favorite 90s flicks.

By using comedy to break the ice, I was able to interact with the group and have an enjoyable conversation. It taught me that sometimes, all it takes is a little comedy to break down boundaries and establish new relationships.

Here are some suggestions on using comedy to break the ice:
Use self-deprecating humor: One method to use comedy is to make fun of yourself. This can demonstrate that you don't take yourself too seriously and can help put others at ease. For

example, you might state "I'm not great at small talk, so I hope you'll bear with me!"

Make a pertinent quip: Another method to use comedy is to make a remark that's relevant to the circumstance or conversation. This can demonstrate that you're paying attention and can help brighten the atmosphere. For example, if you're at a conference, you might remark "I hope the coffee is strong today, we've got a lot of speakers to get through!"

Share a humorous story: If you have an amusing story that's pertinent to the conversation, share it! This can help you interact with others and make them feel more comfortable around you

Engaging in Small Talk
Small chat is an important talent in perfecting the art of communication, particularly when it comes to conversing with ladies. Here are some suggestions to help you participate in a casual talk:

Start with a sincere compliment: Everyone loves to be acknowledged. A genuine compliment can be a wonderful ice-breaker and help you establish a relationship.

Listen actively: Pay attention to what the other individual is saying and respond appropriately. Active attention demonstrates that you are interested in the conversation and the other individual.

Don't be scared of silence: Silence is not always a negative thing. Sometimes, it can be an opportunity to ruminate on the conversation and think of new topics to speak about.

Some of the perfect short chat conversations

Person A: Hi, how are you doing?

Person B: I'm doing fairly well, thanks for inquiring. How about you?

Person A: I'm doing well too, gracias. I observed you're carrying an instrument case. Do you play?

Person B: Yeah, I'm actually on my way to a job right now. I perform in a neighborhood ensemble.

Person A: Oh, that's really amazing. What kind of songs do you people play?

Person B: We perform a blend of rock and blues. It's been really enjoyable to experiment with different designs.

Person A: I've always respected persons who can perform instruments. I can scarcely sustain a melody. How did you get started?

Person B: My dad played guitar when I was growing up, so I started playing with him when I was small. I've been playing ever since.

Person A: That's amazing. Do you compose your own music too?

Person B: Yeah, I do. It's one of my greatest aspects of performing music.

Person A: That's really remarkable. I've always been captivated by the artistic process. What's your strategy for composing music?

Person B: I typically start with a rhythm or a harmonic arrangement and develop from there. Sometimes I'll have a particular concept or motif in mind, but other times it just comes together as I experiment around with different ideas.

Person A: That's really fascinating. It sounds like a really gratifying artistic release. Thanks for sharing that with me.

Person B: Of course, thanks for asking. What about you? Do you have any interests or artistic activities that you enjoy?

Finding Common Ground
is an important element of successful communication and conflict settlement. When

two or more individuals have contrasting viewpoints or beliefs, it can be challenging to come to a consensus or find a solution that satisfies everyone. However, by recognizing common ground, individuals can work towards a shared objective and achieve a mutually advantageous solution.

Chapter 4: Navigating Challenging Conversations

Challenging conversations can be uncomfortable and challenging, but they are essential for healthy relationships and effective communication. Whether it's confronting a problem with a colleague, discussing a sensitive subject with a loved one, or negotiating a business transaction, navigating challenging conversations requires tolerance, ability, and subtlety.

Here are some techniques for navigating challenging conversations:

Set the tone: Begin the conversation by establishing an optimistic tone. Establish an open and considerate environment by acknowledging the other person's perspective and communicating your desire to find a mutually satisfactory solution.

Listen actively: Active attention is important during challenging conversations. It includes completely concentrating on the other person's words and attempting to comprehend their perspective without criticism or interference. By observing attentively, you can better comprehend the other person's problems, motivations, and beliefs.

Communicate clearly: Communicate your thoughts and emotions in a straightforward and succinct fashion. Avoid forming generalizations or rushing to conclusions. Instead, ask clarification inquiries to ensure that you have a complete comprehension of the other person's perspective.

Use "I" statements: When addressing sensitive subjects, it can be simple to become protective or aggressive. Using "I" expressions, such as "I feel" or, "I think," can help you communicate your concerns without putting the responsibility on the other individual.

Practice empathy: Try to comprehend the other person's perspective and emotions. Put yourself in their position and contemplate how you would feel in their predicament. By exercising sensitivity, you can create a stronger relationship and discover a mutually advantageous solution.

Take pauses if needed: If feelings are running high or the conversation becomes too challenging, it's acceptable to take a break. Take some time to ruminate and recover before returning to the conversation with a clear mind

Awkward situations are unavoidable in conversations. They can happen when we say something that offends the other person, or when we simply run out of things to say. However, it's essential to manage these circumstances graciously in order to avoid making matters worse.

Here are some suggestions for managing uncomfortable situations in a conversation:

Don't panic: The first stage is to remain cool and prevent screaming. Awkward situations are a natural component of conversations, and they happen to everyone. Take a long inhalation and attempt to unwind.

Acknowledge the embarrassment: It's often beneficial to acknowledge the awkwardness of the circumstance. You can say something like, "Well, that was awkward," or "I'm not sure what to say now." This can help to break the tension and demonstrate to the other individual that you're conscious of the circumstance.

Change the subject: If the conversation has become uncomfortable due to a sensitive topic or miscommunication, it's often best to change the subject. You can ask the other individual a question about a different subject, or make a lighthearted statement to brighten the atmosphere.

Apologize if necessary: If you've said something that has insulted the other individual, it's essential to apologize. Be genuine and accept accountability for your remarks. Say something like, "I'm sorry, that was insensitive of me," or "I didn't mean to offend you."

Use humor: Humor can be a wonderful way to alleviate an uncomfortable circumstance. You can make a jest or share a humorous story to relieve the atmosphere. Just be cautious not to use comedy in a way that could be seen as insulting or inappropriate.

Take a pause: Sometimes, the best way to manage an uncomfortable situation is to take a break from the conversation. Excuse yourself to use the bathroom or get a glass of water. This can offer both you and the other individual an opportunity to compose your thoughts and recover

The do's and don'ts of flirting

Do's:

Start with a smile: A welcoming smile can immediately generate a favorable impression and make you more approachable.

Be confident: Confidence is attractive, so make sure you're comfortable in your own flesh and reflect that in your relationships.

Use humor: Humor can brighten the atmosphere and make both parties feel more relaxed and comfortable.

Listen actively: Pay attention to what the other individual is saying and respond in a considerate and interesting manner. This demonstrates that you're enthusiastic and involved in the conversation.

commendation sincerely: A well-placed commendation can make someone feel good about themselves and open them up to further conversation.

Don'ts:

Don't be too aggressive: Pushing too hard or coming on too forceful can be off-putting and make the other individual uncomfortable.

Don't disregard boundaries: Respect personal space and boundaries, and be conscious of what the other individual is comfortable with.

Don't make inappropriate comments: Avoid commenting on someone's physical attractiveness in a manner that could be perceived as insulting or inappropriate.

Don't be disrespectful: Being impolite or indifferent towards someone is a significant turn-off and will likely stop any possibility of further interaction.

Don't be too anxious: While it's essential to demonstrate curiosity, being too eager or dependent can come across as desperate and turn the other person off.

Difference between flirtation and harassment
Flirting and harassment are two separate behaviors that can be easily mistaken, but it's essential to understand the difference to ensure that you're not breaking any boundaries or making anyone feel uncomfortable.

Flirting is a consenting and reciprocal act of demonstrating emotional or erotic interest in someone, typically through lighthearted conversation, compliments, and non-threatening physical contact. It's a positive and considerate method to communicate your attraction to someone and is pleasurable for both parties involved.

On the other hand, harassment is a non-consensual behavior that includes relentless and unwelcome approaches, inappropriate statements, or physical contact that makes the other person feel uncomfortable, intimidated, or disrespected. It's an unfavorable and disrespectful behavior that can cause emotional discomfort, anxiety, or trauma.

Examples of flirtation could include:

Starting a conversation with a compliment: "Hi, I just wanted to say that I think you have a great smile."

Using lighthearted banter: "So, are you always this charming, or are you just putting it on for me?"

Asking someone out on a date: "Hey, I was wondering if you'd like to grab a drink with me sometime?"

Examples of intimidation could include:

Making inappropriate statements about someone's appearance: "Wow, you look fantastic today. I'd adore taking you home with me."

Touching someone without their consent: "Hey, I just wanted to feel your musculature. You appear so powerful."

Following someone around or turning up at their workplace or residence uninvited: "I just can't stop thinking about you. I had to see you again."

It's essential to note that the distinction between flirting and harassment can be subjective and depends on the individual's perspective and comfort level. If someone informs you that they're not interested or that your behavior is making them uncomfortable, it's essential to observe their boundaries and cease the behavior immediately.

Reading the body expression
This is an essential element of social interaction, as it can provide valuable information about someone's emotions, motivations, and attitudes. Here are some suggestions on how to interpret body language and what to do in different situations:

Observe facial expressions: Facial expressions can disclose a lot about someone's feelings, such as contentment, wrath, melancholy, or astonishment. Pay attention to the forehead, cheeks, and eyes, as they can indicate whether someone is comfortable, involved, or disinterested. If someone's facial expression indicates uneasiness or dissatisfaction, it's essential to acknowledge that and attempt to understand why.

Notice body position: Body posture can communicate confidence, aggressiveness, or uneasiness. If someone is standing or sitting up straight, establishing eye contact, and addressing you squarely, it's an indication that they are involved and interested in the conversation. On the other hand, if someone is slouching, averting eye contact, or looking away from you, it could indicate indifference, discomfort, or even animosity.

Pay attention to gestures: Gestures, such as hand movements or restlessness, can disclose anxiousness, anxiety, or irritation. If someone is fiddling with their hair, rubbing their foot, or chewing their nails, it could indicate that they are uncomfortable or impatient. If you observe these behaviors, it's essential to attempt to resolve the circumstance and make the individual feel more comfortable.

Consider background: Body language can be influenced by the circumstances of the situation. For example, someone may display apprehension or uneasiness in a job application or a first meeting. In these circumstances, it's essential to be conscious of the power relations and attempt to help the other individual feel more comfortable.

Respond appropriately: Once you've read someone's body language, it's essential to respond appropriately. If someone seems uncomfortable or disinterested, it's essential to acknowledge that and modify your behavior appropriately. You can attempt to redirect the subject or ask them inquiries to interest them further. On the other hand, if someone is displaying positive body language, such as beaming and making eye contact, it's an indication that they are involved and interested, and you can respond by continuing the conversation and expressing interest in them.

Sending the correct indication

Sending the correct indication is essential in social circumstances, as it can help you communicate your objectives and create a favorable impression on others. However, it's also essential to convey the indication in a manner that is confident and authentic, without coming across as uncomfortable or dishonest. Here are some suggestions on how to convey the correct indication without appearing stupid:

Be explicit about your objectives: Before delivering a communication, it's essential to be clear about your intentions and what you expect to communicate. Are you attempting to demonstrate an interest in someone romantically, or merely trying to establish a pleasant conversation? Being explicit about your objectives will help you convey the correct indication and prevent any misunderstandings.

Use body language: Body language can be an effective method to convey the correct indication. For example, standing up straight, establishing eye contact, and beaming can communicate confidence and friendliness. On the other hand, crossing your arms or averting eye contact can communicate uneasiness or indifference. It's essential to be conscious of your body language and how it may be interpreted by others.

Use verbal signals: Verbal cues, such as compliments or instigating conversation, can also be a method to convey the correct indication. However, it's essential to use these signals in a manner that is sincere and authentic. For example, instead of using a typical pickup line, attempt to instigate a conversation about something that sincerely interests you or something you have in common.

Be considerate: It's essential to convey the correct indication in a manner that is respectful of the other person's boundaries and emotions. Avoid making conclusions or coming on too aggressively, and be mindful of behavioral signals that may indicate uneasiness or indifference. If someone seems uncomfortable, it's essential to back off and observe their boundaries.

Be confident: Finally, it's essential to convey the correct indication with confidence and truthfulness. Instead of attempting to put on Assà noa character or behave in a certain manner, be yourself and let your personality radiate through. Remember that everyone gets anxious or feels uncomfortable sometimes and that it's acceptable to be vulnerable and authentic

.

Chapter 5: Enhancing Your Communication Skills

Effective communication is a crucial component of achievement in both domestic and professional situations. Whether it's chatting with colleagues, delivering demonstrations, or having conversations with friends and family, the ability to communicate successfully is important. However, communication is a talent that requires exercise and improvement. In this chapter, we will explore some methods to improve your communication abilities.

Verbal Communication
Verbal communication includes communicating plainly, succinctly, and with conviction. It's essential to use appropriate vocabulary and tone when speaking to others and to be conscious of nonverbal signals such as body language and facial expressions. Practice conversing in front of a reflection or with a trustworthy

acquaintance or associate to enhance your speech communication skills.

Written Communication

Written communication is just as essential as direct communication, particularly in professional situations. It's essential to write plainly and succinctly, using appropriate language and capitalization. When composing letters, make sure to proofread your content before submitting it. If you're not positive about something, don't be hesitant to inquire for clarification.

Emotional Intelligence

Emotional intelligence is the capacity to recognize and comprehend feelings in yourself and others. It involves the capacity to control your own feelings, sympathize with others, communicate successfully, and create powerful relationships. Emotional intelligence is a crucial ability for success in personal and professional relationships, as it can help you negotiate social circumstances, work successfully with others, and make better decisions.

There are several components of emotional intelligence, including:
Self-awareness: This includes comprehending your own feelings, recognizing how they influence your behavior, and determining your abilities and limitations.
Self-regulation: This includes controlling your feelings and instincts, preventing impetuous actions, and adjusting to shifting circumstances.

Motivation: This includes establishing objectives, working towards them, and persevering in the face of difficulties.
Empathy: This includes comprehending and empathizing with the feelings of others, identifying their perspectives, and communicating successfully.
Social skills: This includes establishing relationships, working successfully with others, and encouraging others to accomplish shared objectives.

Allow me to meander a little bit. If you are here then you might have received some information about the craft of communication, now let's assume you are now in an intimate relationship these will be helpful:

Achieving success in a personal relationship can be a gratifying and fulfilling experience. While every relationship is distinct, there are some important components that can help you establish a healthy and enduring connection with your companion. Here are some suggestions for attaining success in your intimate relationship:

Trust: Trust is important for establishing a powerful and enduring relationship. This means being dependable and consistent in your actions, being forthright, and maintaining your commitments. It also means offering your companion the benefit of the doubt and allowing them to do the same for you.

Respect: Mutual respect is another essential ingredient of a successful relationship. This means handling your companion with compassion, sensitivity, and consideration, even when you disagree or have different perspectives. It also means understanding your partner's boundaries, viewpoints, and emotions.

Quality time: Spending quality time together is essential for establishing a strong emotional relationship with your companion. This means creating time for each other, participating in activities you both appreciate and being present and receptive when you are together.

Compromise: Relationships require compromise and finding a medium ground that works for both partners. This means being adaptable and open-minded and prepared to compromise on things that are not important to your fundamental principles or beliefs.

Support: Supporting your companion through happy times and negative is essential for developing a healthy and enduring relationship. This means being there for them emotionally, physically, and psychologically, and encouraging their objectives and aspirations.

Practice, practice, practice

Improving your communication abilities requires exercise. Look for opportunities to exercise your abilities in everyday circumstances. This could be as straightforward as having a conversation with an acquaintance or family member or participating in a public speaking group. The more you exercise, the more confident and successful you will become

Speak plainly and confidently

When you communicate, do so plainly and confidently. Use a powerful, distinct voice and avoid muttering or speaking too rapidly. Speak at a comfortable speed and pause periodically to allow the audience time to process what you are saying. Pay attention to your body expression and make sure it represents what you are saying.

Using Technology to your Advantage

Technology can be an effective instrument for improving your communication skills, both in domestic and professional situations. Here are some methods you can use technology to your advantage:

Video conferencing: With the increase of distant work and virtual gatherings, video conferencing tools like Zoom, Microsoft Teams, and Skype have become important for efficient collaboration. These tools enable you to have face-to-face conversations with individuals, no matter where they are situated. They also enable you to share displays and communicate on documents in real time.

Social media: Social media platforms like LinkedIn, Twitter, and Facebook can be used to develop professional networks and interact with new individuals. These platforms enable you to share changes, interact with others, and learn about business trends and events.

Email: Email is a conventional but still important communication instrument. Make sure your letters are straightforward and succinct, with a particular subject line and a courteous and professional tone.

Messaging applications: Messaging apps like WhatsApp and Slack can be used for rapid and informal communication These applications enable you to exchange communications, share information, and collaborate on projects in real time.

Speech recognition tools: Speech recognition tools like Dragon Naturally Speaking can help you enhance your speech communication abilities. These tools enable you to transcribe text, emails, or documents, which can be particularly beneficial for those who struggle with coding or have an impairment.

In conclusion, understanding the art of conversation and communication is a talent that can serve you well throughout your life, both individually and professionally. Throughout this book, we have examined various elements of successful communication, including active attention, precision, behavioral signals, and adaptability.

In particular, we have addressed the significance of communicating with women appropriately and professionally, without any gender prejudice or discrimination. It is important to concentrate on establishing powerful relationships with women based on reciprocal respect and comprehension.

By following the guidelines and techniques described in this book, you can become a better conversationalist, able to communicate with ladies and people from all areas of life. Remember that successful communication is a continual process, and it requires continuous exercise and self-reflection.

As you progress forward in your adventure of perfecting the art of conversation and communication, I challenge you to continue to learn and develop, seek feedback, and be receptive to new ideas and perspectives. By doing so, you will be well on your way to becoming a competent communicator and establishing powerful, significant relationships with the ladies in your life.